Mastering Canine Communication

The Power of The.Quiet.Kue™

I0111971

by
Jennifer Broome

TREMENDOUS
LEADERSHIP
Leadership with a kick!

Tremendous Leadership
PO Box 267 • Boiling Springs, PA 17007
(717) 701 - 8159 • (800) 233 - 2665
www.TremendousLeadership.com

Paperback ISBN: 978-1-961202-13-9
Hardcover ISBN: 978-1-961202-18-4
eBook ISBN: 978-1-961202-14-6

Back cover author photo by Shaileen English

DESIGNED & PRINTED IN THE
UNITED STATES OF AMERICA

TABLE OF CONTENTS

ACKNOWLEDGEMENTS

One of the most influential mentors in my dog training career has been Mr. Rick Smith. I attended my first Huntsmith Seminar back in the early 2000s. Nearly ten years later, with a shaky, nervous voice and butterflies in my stomach, I called Mr. Smith to explain the problem that I was experiencing. I was a professional dog trainer about ten years into my career. I had already built my booming Quinebaug Kennels business and was enjoying early success; however, something about the dogs and the people seemed to be shifting, and I needed help!

I noticed alarming changes as I expanded my business to accept family pet and companion dog training. While I had been highly involved with my sporting dog clients, helping them seek the best genetics and guiding them through the puppy process, the culture shifted with the newer generations of dog enthusiasts adopting all-positive reinforcement and training methods. Dogs were becoming more spoiled, enabled, and indulged, even in the gun dog world, with dogs showing up at my kennel emotionally wrecked.

Recognizing the need for change, Rick was just the person I needed! Rick could not have been more helpful and caring as he listened to my struggles and offered unending lessons. His wisdom enabled me to realize the source of the challenging canine behavior and what I needed to address and modify to help these dogs and their owners best. Inviting Rick to Quinebaug Kennels to host his Huntsmith clinics significantly impacted me. From that interaction forward, Rick's teachings and mentorship with The Foundation Training helped me change my standards, understand principles, and hold dogs to higher levels, making me a better trainer. Quinebaug Kennels serves as the foundation and inspiration for The.Quiet.Kue™, intertwining the initials and essence of the kennel's name into a method focused on understanding and quiet communication with dogs. With Rick's mentorship, I adopted, practiced, and revised his teachings to navigate my customers and their dogs.

Learning from Rick through seminars and phone calls, I gained detailed insights into dog behavior, body language, and quiet communication. Rick's humility and dedication to passing on his knowledge inspired me to share the training methods in this book. It's my honor to share The.Quiet.Kue™, hoping these methods will help others better understand and communicate with their dogs. I owe much of my success to Rick and am honored to call him a friend. Thank you.

Jennifer Broome

DEDICATION

To the Wonderlead

Dedicating a book to a dog leash might seem unconventional, but the Wonderlead, crafted by Mr. Delmar Smith, stands as one of the greatest innovations in dog training. Its unique design, with a slip-style stiffness that creates a definitive noise just before engaging pressure, provides a crucial tool in teaching both dogs and their handlers. The Wonderlead doesn't just guide dogs; it teaches handlers to communicate effectively through light touch and empathy, fostering mutual understanding and respect. Through the wisdom and mentorship of Rick Smith, I've learned to navigate the complexities of canine behavior and communication, paving the way for a more compassionate and effective approach to training. The Wonderlead isn't just a tool; it's a symbol of the transformative power of light touch and understanding in the world of dog training.

Quinebaug's Sweet Filly In The Ferns MH "Filly" at The Labrador Retriever Club fall hunt test in Connecticut, where she titled achieving her Master Hunter status by passing 6 out of 6 separate AKC tests over the course of a year.

FOREWORD BY RICK SMITH

Allow me to introduce you to Jennifer Broome, a woman of remarkable talents and unyielding dedication. Jennifer operates a comprehensive establishment, encompassing kennel services, training, breeding, and grooming. Her vision spans across various domains, yet she remains remarkably humble and free of any egotistical tendencies. Jennifer's pursuits are driven by an unwavering commitment to her beliefs, and she tirelessly chases her passions.

This book is crafted to reach those who share a profound love for working with dogs and aspire to lead them in the most effective manner. Jennifer's approach rejects indulgence or pampering of animals, emphasizing discipline and structure instead. What sets Jennifer apart is her extraordinary ability to educate not only dogs but also people. With decades of observation and interaction with both dogs and their human counterparts, she has developed a profound understanding of crafting successful collaborations and communication.

Jennifer's openness to innovative approaches sets her apart. Her primary concern is the welfare of her clients and their dogs, continuously seeking ways to enhance their lives. Her motivation is pure and rooted in a deep passion for her work. She is a dedicated student of her craft, fully endorsing her methodology. Jennifer possesses an unparalleled level of expertise in her field.

Jennifer radiates confidence in her expertise, and she's eager to share her game plan with you and your dog through this book. Her authority and influence over dogs are extraordinary. She will teach you that, once you take charge, your dog will find comfort in following your lead. This book is your gateway to acquiring answers from an experienced, hands-on trainer. Jennifer provides the necessary resources for you to achieve your goals. She emphasizes the role of mentorship, guiding you to become a leader, not just for your dog but also for yourself. Dogs crave a leader, and Jennifer will empower you to fill that role.

For those seeking insights from a seasoned and professional trainer, this book provides a wealth of knowledge. Jennifer will show you that, indeed, you can address and rectify various issues, but you must be prepared to put in the effort. Her guidance equips you to become an effective mentor, first for yourself and then for your dog. Dogs seek a trustworthy leader, and you are about to embark on a journey to become precisely that under Jennifer's guidance.

Rick Smith is a trainer, clinician, competitor, breeder, writer, American Brittany Club Hall of Fame inductee, and current (2023) President of Bird Dog Foundation, Inc.

INTRODUCTION

Look at most people at the other end of a dog's leash, and you will see the problem. It is most often not the dog but the hands of the human unfairly restraining it for no reason. There is no release of pressure; instead, there is constant pressure with a tight leash. The dog pulls, so the human pulls and holds. With continuous, invasive, and claustrophobic pressure, the dogs cannot seek relief, so they pull even harder.

People often hold onto their personal baggage when holding onto a dog. Rather than be "in the moment," they stress about the last time their dog reacted to another dog, so they now bear down and hold pressure in anticipation, when in reality, this just cues the dog that something IS WRONG! The human needs to own their stuff. If you choose to live in safe harmony and respect around an animal, you need to be clear. Be the Leader, or the animal will lead.

Time and time again, there are new inventions to stop a dog from pulling when, sadly, it is the human pulling, clenching, and holding tight! Here are some examples of the more common training devices: There are face halters that strap to the sensitive bridges of dogs' noses. There are innovative no-pull harnesses that either compress a dog's shoulder, restricting movement or lift their armpits up and outward, forcing them into an uncomfortable and damaging position. There are comfortable padded shoulder harnesses that often encourage pulling. There are choke chains that choke and prong collars that pinch. I even recently saw an electronic collar attached to a leash that, when you pulled, applied stimulation automatically.

> When the human holds the leash without intent or with fear, anger, or frustration, the dog becomes reactive.

Besides the no-pull harnesses (which sports medicine guru and canine athlete enthusiast Dr. Chris Zink explains are detrimental to a dog's structure and gait because they constrict proper movement and leg extension and cause dogs to bear less weight on their outside leg), the other options mentioned can and do have a wonderful place in training. Unfortunately, the methodology is based more on blaming the dog for the action of pulling; therefore, they suffer the consequence of the device when, in reality, it is the human who pulls and does not stop (Whole Dog Journal, 2013).

> You get more with less! Try less force, less invasive devices, and more teaching.

This book's methodology and teaching system is called The.Quiet.Kue™. It is highly specialized and wonderfully proven through our Quinebaug Kennels training system. I developed this system through my years of learning while training dogs professionally, training my horses, and integrating other very successful training methods into a refined and unique system that brought lightness, communication, and partnership to my current dog training program. For nearly 12 years my team has integrated this program with hundreds of dogs each year. I have personally trained thousands of dogs over my 30-year career and learned more from the dogs than they ever learned from me.

This is not just a training book; it is a dive into a methodology and thought process that teaches you to understand the dog's mind before mechanically trying to teach or enforce obedience. I am explaining behavior and learning to learn. Wanting to learn to learn because you not only take the leash to demonstrate leadership, but you earn trust and gain partnership though becoming a Leader in which your dog desires to willingly follow.

> **We MUST be our dog's leaders,
> not for US, but for THEM.**

POINT OF CONTACT

POC, or Point of Contact, is a physical connection. When working with animals, POC is employed in various ways to communicate and teach them. Since animals do not have an innate natural understanding of oral communication with words, it is essential to instruct them in a manner they can comprehend.

Body language is paramount in canine communication, serving as a primary mode of interaction between dogs and humans. Dogs are highly attuned to visual cues, making body language a fundamental aspect of their social dynamics. However, dogs are also highly in tune with our blood pressure, heart rate, smell, and energy. In truth, we are all a part of a complex animal kingdom. If humans take the time to be IN THE MOMENT more, read their dogs, and communicate non-verbally, they will often find even more accurate communication occurring. While force is a commonly misunderstood approach, relying solely on it oversimplifies the intricate dialogue between humans and dogs.

The more you FORCE an animal to comply, the less they try. The more work you do, the less effort they give. Teach with lightness and politeness and provide them with the problem-solving skills to learn to willingly follow light cues.

Understanding canine body language allows for more nuanced and compelling communication. Gentle cues and a receptive, confident posture establish trust, fostering a deeper connection. Handlers can engage in a dialogue that respects the dog's natural instincts and promotes a harmonious relationship based on mutual understanding and cooperation by emphasizing non-verbal signals and avoiding reliance on force.

One fundamental principle is the concept of pressure versus the release of pressure or discomfort versus comfort. It's important to note that this concept does not necessarily involve applying force to the point of pain. The ultimate goal is to get our dogs to listen to our commands and teach them in a language they understand. Think of leash pressure as a stimulus and the release of leash pressure as the reward. Dogs do not learn from the pressure; they learn from the RELEASE of pressure.

In recent years, society has been trending toward force-free or positive-only training methods, often viewing pressure-based training as undesirable. This shift parallels broader societal changes, including a decline in respect for authority figures and institutions.

Interestingly, this societal shift is reflected in canine behavior, with increased aggression observed in dogs that have become defiant when asked to perform simple tasks.

> When the humans are not consistent, the dogs are not consistent. Our dog's true bond and willingness to follow us is a behavior based on the animal respecting the human. Most people don't want to be TOLD anything; therefore, they don't want their dog to be told!

These dogs may react with a fight, freeze, or flight reaction when truly demanded to perform a task, most often because they have never been made to do something. Their reaction is simply a form of resistance. Examples include trimming their nails, accepting a veterinarian exam politely, or needing to climb stairs. When the dog has not been exposed to tasks with a methodology that encompasses that they MUST comply, the outcome of resistance is often intense and emotional based on fear, confusion, lack of confidence, or just unwillingness.

All people slip. We get lazy, busy, and inconsistent. Then the dog slips, too. Sadly, dogs' lack of rules, structure, and discipline may only cause the animal to spiral down a path of failure. Unruliness quickly becomes aggression, and ill-behaved dogs only live more isolated lives, or worse yet, get relinquished to shelters or even more dreadful outcomes. Let's face it: good dogs get to go places and enjoy a life of even greater enrichment. It is wonderful to be around a well-mannered, well-behaved dog!

Animals inherently understand and respond to pressure and release even better than humans. Here are some examples: A dog lying in the sun experiences discomfort as the sun's heat intensifies (pressure/discomfort). The dog responds by moving to the shade, seeking relief and comfort (release of pressure). When a dog investigates a cat and encounters aggressive signals such as hissing and swatting (pressure), the dog backs away to avoid confrontation and seek comfort (release of pressure).

Teaching a young puppy to sit by gently lifting its collar to raise its head and placing two fingers (index and thumb in a squeezing action) on its rump to apply gentle pressure is a simple form of pressure and release training. In response, puppies instinctively move into or with the pressure and seek the release of pressure, thereby learning the desired behavior.

In essence, pressure is any form of force or stimulus that creates mental or physical awareness, stress, influence, or discomfort.

> ## The instant release of pressure leads to comfort, signifying the correct response.

The success of these methods is attributed to the deep understanding and learning that comes from observing and interacting with dogs. While various training approaches and resources are available, the most valuable insights come directly from dogs and their natural behaviors. Here are some critical reasons for the success of these methods:

Learning from the Source: The best coaches and mentors in dog training are the dogs themselves. Rather than relying solely on online courses, scientific databases, or behavioral experts, I have chosen to immerse myself in the world of dogs and observe their behavior firsthand. While I have had the privilege of studying with some of the best trainers in the industry, the dogs are my constant source of learning. Dog training is not a skill you can learn solely from reading a book or taking an online course.

When you can get your hands on hundreds and even thousands of dogs of all ages, breeds, temperaments, and energy levels, those are the dogs that take you to school. You learn from your failures and build upon your successes. You assemble a toolbox of methods that enable you to respond to nearly every action a dog can display.

Each dog is a complete individual, and various minute tweaks can be implemented to achieve even more successful communication. And often, the more challenging the dog, the more lessons you can learn. I learn from the dogs themselves every day.

Sometimes, we must be tough. Sometimes, it is just going to hurt. When we bounce a check, the fee hurts. When we speed and get an expensive ticket, it hurts. Sometimes, you must tell a dog, "That is NOT allowed."

Observing Body Language: I've spent years paying close attention to the subtle cues and body language displayed by dogs. This includes ear movements, eyes, facial expressions, tail position, interactions with other dogs, reactions to various stimuli, posture, movement patterns, and more. These non-verbal forms of communication among dogs convey a wealth of information.

Understanding Canine Communication: Dogs communicate with each other through various actions and behaviors. What may appear as a dog fight to humans is often a quick and decisive demonstration of dominant behavior, with one dog correcting another. Actual dog fights, where dogs are evenly matched in pack status, can be extremely dangerous and even deadly. These insights into canine social dynamics help build these training methods.

Importance of Early Socialization: I need to emphasize the critical role of early socialization in teaching dogs proper social skills. Puppies interacting with each other and their mother provide valuable lessons in how dogs instinctively respond to stimulus, pressure, and the release of pressure. These early experiences shape a dog's understanding of social hierarchies and communication.

The most stressful time in a puppy's life is when their Mom cuts them off from nursing. When their teeth start to come in, and she has had enough, she will growl at them, snap, pin, and bite if necessary. She is done, and the message is loud and clear. She is not always careful, and she is downright rough at times. She teaches them to understand and respect fear.

Respecting Canine Language: Shift away from human-centric, verbal communication and instead study, understand, and appreciate the language of dogs. Dogs have a rich and nuanced way of communicating with each other, which often goes unnoticed by humans. By paying attention to these signals and cues, humans can better connect with and train their dogs effectively.

Have you ever truly studied your dog's body language to observe that your dog is acknowledging your communication and is in a thinking state of mind? When dogs are focused and open to learning, they respond with subtle yet definitive replies to your communication. Signs of their engagement with you include blinking, licking their lips, swallowing, and yawning. Their ear posture may be back and attentive or up and engaged with you. A dog genuinely pays all their attention to you if they have their ears and eyes on you. When a dog is willing, they are receptive to your communication.

They may also be looking away at their surroundings (still keeping track of you with hyper-aware backward ear poses). If their eyes and ears are focused on something else, they are not engaged with you. They are focused on something else and are most likely not thinking and responding to your cues. They are distracted.

In summary, the success of my methods lies in my deep immersion in the world of dogs and my commitment to learning from dogs themselves. By observing and understanding canine behavior, body language, and communication, I have practiced effective training approaches that respect dogs' natural instincts and behaviors. Early forms of Point of Contact (POC) in dog training start when puppies are born and continue throughout their early development. These interactions with puppies are designed to help them adapt to human touch, develop resilience, and BUILD COPING MECHANISMS. Here are some key aspects of early POC:

Handling from Birth: Responsible breeders handle newborn puppies from the moment they are born. This interaction includes examining the puppies, checking for any health issues like cleft palates, assisting with the umbilical cord, and gently rubbing the puppies to dry and stimulate them. Daily handling and imprinting, which includes touching and gently stressing the puppies for various examinations, helps condition them to human touch, smell, sound, and interaction.

Early Neurological Stimulation (ENS): Early Neurological Stimulation (ENS) is a crucial set of simple exercises designed to expose puppies to various stressors and stimuli during the critical period from days 3 through 16 of their lives. Research studies, such as those conducted by Dr. Carmen Battaglia, have shown that ENS plays a pivotal role in the development of puppies, enhancing their resilience and coping mechanisms. The positive effects of ENS extend to a puppy's future behavior and adaptability. This is particularly significant for dog trainers and owners, as it helps prevent the development of fear triggers, ultimately contributing to a smoother and more confident canine companion.

Socialization and Stress Exposure: During the first eight weeks of a puppy's life, they should be exposed to various forms of stress, including socialization with human touch, being placed in different positions (such as upside down), undergoing medical procedures like worming and vaccinations, puppy baths, and experiencing nail trimming. Additionally, puppies are often handled and placed in a "stacked" show stance to evaluate their conformation. While these experiences involve stress, they also help condition puppies for future challenges and interactions. They learn early tolerance and acceptance of pressure and stimuli, and often, their efforts to escape or evade are not successful because we can safely subdue and keep them under our control.

POC for Ongoing Training: As puppies reach eight weeks of age and beyond, POC continues to be an essential part of their training. This includes holding puppies in various positions, applying gentle touch to encourage stillness, using touch to guide them into sitting or standing positions, introducing them to crating, acclimating them to nail trimming or a Dremel tool, and teaching them to walk on a leash. POC serves as the area where physical contact is made to elicit a desired response from the puppy, with the instant release of pressure serving as the reward for correct or desired behavior.

The early touch and pressure applied to puppies prepare them for more advanced training tasks and help them develop the ability to handle and navigate various stressors. By learning how to respond to pressure and understanding how to turn it off through desired behavior, puppies gain valuable skills that will serve them throughout their lives. Early POC is a crucial foundation for a dog's ability to adapt, learn, and interact effectively with humans and their environment.

What about those puppies born into unstable environments or lacking the good fortune of being in a sheltered, safe, and healthy situation from birth? Can these puppies ever achieve stability and success? These neglected puppies may start behind, but that doesn't mean they cannot catch up!

We have witnessed numerous rescue dogs adapt to the hand they were dealt, and with nurturing care and appropriate training, these pups can undoubtedly lead balanced, happy, and healthy lives. They may need to contend with adversities later in life, often facing more significant obstacles. It's important to acknowledge that while it's ideal for all puppies to be born into safe and healthy situations, this is frequently not the case. Rather than handicapping these pups by coddling their insecurities and fears or enabling them to remain in an unstable mindset, we have firsthand experience that, with patience, rules, structure, and a strong obedience foundation to learn, these dogs can indeed lead beautiful, enriching, confident, and joyful lives.

THE WONDERLEAD

My preferred training tool is the Wonderlead. I gained extensive knowledge about this unique leash through my 15-plus years of training and mentoring with Rick Smith, son of Delmar Smith, the inventor of the lead. I also had the privilege of working with Delmar and learning training methods with his leash, which gained fame in the bird dog world.

Before delving further, let's explore a brief history of the lead. Developed by Delmar Smith, it originally earned the name "the wonder lead" from another fine trainer, Ed Rader, who exclaimed, "You'll wonder how you ever got along without it." In the Huntsmith program, The Silent Command System, it's referred to as the Command Lead. Regardless of the name, it stands as an invaluable training tool.

> The Wonderlead was created by the Smith Family in the 1980s after working animals on "The King Ranch."

The stiffness of the lasso command lead is its primary benefit. This stiff rope, akin to a piggin string used by cowhands for tying cattle by the feet, allows for a spring-like action as soon as your hand lets go. Due to the round rope release, the cessation of stimulation is immediate. When reward is quick, the dog learns more easily what is expected. The Huntsmith website emphasizes that a soft touch and light hands are crucial.

The Smith Family, renowned in the bird dog world as some of the most famous and legendary trainers of all time, developed the Silent Command System for Bird Dog Training. Recognizing the intelligence of dogs and drawing upon their instincts, this system is synonymous with the Smith family's expertise. Given that words can often confuse dogs, as they were not born understanding a verbal language, the Silent Command System is a powerful method of communication. This foundation is what inspired and shaped The.Quiet.Kue™ system within my Quinebaug Kennels Training Program, acknowledging the effectiveness of silent cues and instinctual communication.

Rick Smith explains that we did not develop this system. Instead, it has been handed down from generation to generation, stemming from 'just being quiet' while training animals. All the good books always told you to be quiet!

The Wonderlead, a preferred training tool, consists of a 6-foot leash made from rigid lariat rope. One end features a knot with a leather stopper, while the other end has a slip-noose-style loop. This loop can be adjusted to fit over the crown of the dog's head, snugly securing it high on the neck just behind the skull. This positioning allows for light pressure control over the dog's head.

One of my favorite aspects of the Wonderlead is that it is uncomfortable on YOUR hands! This leash is rigid and somewhat stiff, unlike supple leather, padded handles, or soft rope leashes, which encourage white-knuckled pressure by human hands. It cues the dog while also prompting the owner to use soft hands and direct and assertive communication—ultimately, just two fingers are used to maneuver and cue the dog.

Wonderlead Basic Operation and Understanding

Out of the package, this stiff lariat rope has a waxed coating and has remained tightly coiled from when it was made. Upon removing from the package, stand firmly on the loop end and give the lead a big stretch up to the sky. If you have bad shoulders or are not tall enough, put the end loop on a fence post or trailer hitch. The goal is to give it one big initial stretch to undo the tightness of the early first coil. Give it a good stretch-out!

When you store the Wonderlead, coil it up with a loop about the size of a basketball. Bending, kinking, or wrapping it in smaller coils compromises its stiff integrity. These leashes can last many years with proper care. Avoid storing them outside in the elements; don't crush or collapse them. Keep them straight while using and coiling to store.

The placement of the Wonderlead goes over the dog's head and up high on their neck just at the base of the back of their skull. This placement gives you the most control, allowing the lightest pressure (as opposed to down lower on the more substantial portions of their necks). If your dog walks on your left side, the long part of the leash should come around the outside of your dog's neck, up and over towards you.

When you put the loop on while facing the dog, it should look like the letter P. If your dog walks on the right side, it is the opposite. This proper placement and application enables the leash to work most effectively to tighten with pressure and instantly release after the leash pressure cue.

Why is this training tool so different from other leashes or training collars? The Wonderlead is a choke-style leash. However, unlike a traditional choke chain, which only opens as long as the chain is long, it is often too big, so it falls to the lower, more muscular portion of a dog's neck and over their windpipe, making them gag and choke! The traditional choke chain placement at the base of the neck and top of their shoulders is desensitized to pressure, and they can pull, choke, grit their teeth, and pull more.

If you tried to use a smaller choke chain so that it would stay up high on the neck, it typically would not be big enough to fit over the crown of the head. Other all-in-one slip lead combinations are often made of soft rope, and while you can use it up higher on the neck, they do not have the same quick-release results as the Wonderlead. They still tend to compress all around universally, and the soft nature does not create a single point of contact spot. This single spot becomes a very important role as we condition to the e-collar.

A prong collar is a widespread training tool. When squeezed, the angle and action of the prongs simulate a dog bite. As discussed earlier, dogs understand pressure and are certainly affected by a bite action! Unfortunately, the clamping and pinching pressure can be very harsh. The sad truth is that if you watch nearly everyone relying on their prong collars, you will see them rarely release the pressure.

> Why do people hold dog leashes so tightly? They must get rid of their baggage and stop gripping the leash so tightly.

So not only does the dog have to endure harsh pressure, but it is often ongoing harsh pressure for no reason. Most are clipped to a wide, heavy leash wrapped around the owner's hands with no regard for the collar's 'bite' severity. These dogs only become even more conditioned to higher pressure and pain levels. Even if used lightly, this training tool is very intense. For specific training, with polite human hands that squeeze slowly, release quickly, and ONLY use pressure to enforce, the prong collar can be a very valuable and effective tool. Unfortunately, rarely do I see them used fairly or properly.

The rigid nature of the Wonderlead explicitly applies pressure at the centric point on the opposite side you are pulling. This means that if the dog is on your left, and you apply a slight, quick tug towards 3 o'clock, the POC (Point of Contact) where the leash touches the dog's neck is on the opposite side at 9 o'clock.

Here is the magic with the Wonderlead! You are using quick yet definitive tugs of the leash, which create a Point of Contact against the neck. The goal is to teach the dog to move **away from** the pressure. The pressure is the enforcer, and the immediate quit of pressure is the instant feedback reward. A reaction that typically works for most dogs is to pull harder (fight), flail away (flight), or stop and do nothing (freeze).

Animals move away from stimulation. So, holding a leash tight only makes them pull harder! Let's stop holding tight.

With patience, persistence, and a repetitive cadence of leash tugs, the moment the dog moves away from the pressure (gives), the tug stops. This process can be prolonged at first, but once they learn to follow your directional cueing tugs, the magic and the lightness happen. The goal is to have the dog follow the directional leash cues up, down, forward, towards, left, and right. These cues later become named commands: go, here, cast right or left, head up to sit, or down to lie down.

THE.QUIET.KUE™

Developed from the bird dog training concept of the Smith family Silent Command System, The.Quiet. Kue™ adopts those cherished methods synonymous with their success with hunting dogs and uses the Wonderlead for all dog breeds and disciplines. We have successfully used the Wonderlead in our training programs at QK for nearly 15 years, teaching every one of our clients how to use the lead. I am honored and proud to share this concept with pet owners, mainly to spread the message that the Smith family has successfully taught within the bird-dog community for over 75 years.

My dear friend and mentor Rick Smith was proud and supportive of my efforts to further share my methodology and evolution of their system. I have introduced the Wonderlead to all my clients, including family pets and companion dogs, seeing how successful the leash and training system was. It became my mission to share this training style for all dogs equally, whether sporting or show, working or companion, regardless of age, breed, or size.

Natural Horsemanship Concepts

The evolution of incorporating Natural Horsemanship into my repertoire took my dog training skills to an entirely new level. It heightened my ability to read subtle body language cues of dogs and respond with patience after they 'spoke' to me—through eye blinking, head drops, licking lips, swallowing, relaxation, and more.

In addition to my extensive studies with the Huntsmith system, I've drawn upon my deep-rooted love and practice of Natural Horse Training, honed over 30 years. Natural Horsemanship, rooted in a kinder and gentler cowboy approach, shares principles that develop rapport with horses. Derived from observing free-roaming horses and rejecting old abusive training methods like breaking a horse, this approach aims to create a partnership rather than a system based on unnecessary force. The primary teaching aid is operant conditioning, reinforcing desired behaviors using a pressure and release system.

What excited me about applying this methodology to dog training is the firsthand experience of its effectiveness in horse training. Being prey species, horses present a more significant challenge, as they are more prone to a flight response. Unlike dogs, you can't simply drag and force a horse due to their massive size. Having learned to be savvy, light, polite, and successful in my horsemanship, partnership, training, and communication with a 1000+ pound flight animal, I realized the transferability of these methods to dogs. Through precise timing, reading the animal, and applying and releasing pressure to elicit a response, adding Natural

Horsemanship concepts to my dog training became a game changer!

> When you can identify and reward the slightest effort from an animal, you are communicating that not only are you rewarding the slightest try, but you are also communicating your awareness of their actions, and you are genuinely paying attention and reading that animal in the moment. You communicate how connected and in tune you are with their slightest movements. The more times you reward even a minimal try, the more you communicate your awareness; often, the result is monumental. Little 'tries' turn into big efforts!

The.Quiet.Kue™ system is a unique communication and training methodology for dogs. Unlike traditional training methods that heavily rely on verbal commands with emotional voice inflections, The.Quiet.Kue™ system prioritizes a nonverbal approach based on light touch and Point of Contact (POC). The objective is to teach dogs specific movements and actions using directive physical cues.

In The.Quiet.Kue™, dogs are trained to respond to subtle touches and cues instead of spoken language. These cues are communicated through physical contact, typically involving light touches or pressures applied at specific POCs on the dog's body. The system aims to convey commands and instructions with minimal verbal communication. We effectively speak their nonverbal language based on body language and apply a stimulus to convey a desired outcome or response.

The core actions that The.Quiet.Kue™ system focuses on are the following:

- **Walk with Me (Heel):** Teaching the dog to walk calmly and closely by the handler's side without pulling on the leash. This is a join-up or partnership.
- **Be Still (Sit, Stand, Lie Down):** Training the dog to assume a calm, still, and composed posture, whether sitting, standing, or lying down.
- **Go Away (Place):** Guiding the dog to move away to a designated location or position.
- **Recall (Come Here):** Teaching the dog to return promptly to the handler upon the recall cue.

The.Quiet.Kue™ system emphasizes calmness, repetition, and partnership. It aims to engage the dog in a focused, relaxed, tranquil, and stable state of mind, as opposed to anxiety, excitement, hyperactivity, antagonism, fear, or aggression. The goal of maintaining a calm and quiet demeanor as a handler is to guide the dog to respond to The.Quiet.Kue™ cues.

People need to get themselves into a calm mindset.

First, they must get rid of their baggage (stress, fear, frustration, anger, worry), then be in the moment and train the dog they have today. Each training session should start with a clean slate and build upon previous lessons.

Escape, bolting, freezing, or fighting behaviors are part of the RESISTANCE phase. These reactions are initially discouraged and redirected through nurturing, teaching, and guidance using non-verbal cues and consequences. The system promotes a partnership between the handler and the dog, where communication primarily relies on these non-verbal light cues.

Once the dog has consistently responded to The. Quiet.Kue™ cues through repetition, respect, teaching, and guidance, specific verbal names (e.g., sit, place, here) may be assigned to each action. However, it's essential to remember that the dog's understanding of body language actions remains paramount even when using verbal commands. The.Quiet.Kue™ system strongly emphasizes respecting the dog's perspective and focusing on non-verbal communication to foster a harmonious partnership between humans and dogs. The owner/trainer/handler learns to focus on and study the dog's body language just as much as the dog naturally studies our body language.

Establishing and using Point of Contact (POC) with the leash is a fundamental aspect of communication and obedience in dog training. It helps create a strong partnership between the handler and the dog, enabling clear communication and desired behaviors. Here's a breakdown of how POC is utilized in various training tasks:

POC "Heel" or Walk with Me (The Working Walk): The goal here is to have the dog walk attentively by the handler's side, referred to as "heeling." Establishing this side position as the dog's comfort zone is vital. A working walk should be a partnership, leadership, and bonding time. The handler becomes the driver, and the dog follows, mimicking movements, stops and turns. This level of engagement requires concentration, problem-solving decisions, and engagement from the dog. This responsibility feeds their brains and nourishes the need to work. The dogs become satiated by delving deep into their thinking minds.

POC Be Still: This aspect of training focuses on teaching the dog to sit, lie down, or stand still while in a desired location. The leash neck POC guides the dog into the desired sitting, down, or standing posture. The Be Still focuses on teaching a dog to compose themselves with calmness while being greeted, touched, or handled. It is especially valuable for sporting dogs for steadiness work to sit or whoa/stand still.

When we STOP, we initially teach with a leash cue. The dog's job is to stop. Teaching your dog to stop, be still, and control its emotions encompasses the all-important task of being calm and composed. The more still a dog is, the more stable it is.

POC Go to Place: This training teaches the dog to move away from the handler to a specific, identifiable spot, often called "place" training. It's particularly useful for commands like "go to bed" at home or "go quest/hunt" in the field. The neck POC cues guide the dog to the designated location. This destination training is very identifiable to a dog and gives them a specific target with precise information.

POC Recall or Come to Me: The recall cue, often referred to as "come to me" or simply "here," is crucial for safety and obedience. It involves using the neck POC to draw the dog toward the handler. This command is essential both in everyday situations and in the field. It can mean returning to the handler, coming close, or completing a retrieve task.

What benefits the dog? Teach them skills to help make their lives better! They must live in our world, and training helps them to navigate better within our society. People enjoy being around good dogs. Well-trained dogs live more fulfilled lives.

Starting the Point of Contact (POC) Journey

Let's introduce leash training using a systematic approach incorporating leash-to-neck touch communication, precise timing, and body language. This method serves as a valuable tool for introducing Point of Contact (POC) to new dogs and reconditioning dogs that have developed a habit of pulling on the leash. Once you've committed to ending the practice of holding the leash tightly and allowing your dog to pull, it's essential to consistently implement this new method every time you find yourself at the other end of the leash. It's necessary to recognize that dogs pull because of the continuous pressure you exert by holding tightly and bracing against their pull. To help them learn, they must experience the release of pressure. This training can begin as early as eight weeks with a patient and gentle technique, even with puppies.

Attention Drill

Full Leash Length: The best and most successful approach is to start in a low-distraction area like your backyard. Begin by giving the dog 6 feet of leash, holding the end with just one hand at the leather stopper. Insert the stopper through your fore and middle fingers, with the end at the palm side. Using the full length of the leash is crucial, avoiding unnecessary gathering or holding in the middle with your free hand, which can limit the dog's movement.

Start walking: Anytime the dog gets to the end of the leash and tries to pull, change directions.

You must portray leadership when walking a dog on the leash! Dogs are attached to you and can feel all of your emotions. They can read your lack of confidence if you are hesitant, passive, or unsure. So, grasp onto the leash and GO SOMEWHERE!

Direction Change: Whenever the dog starts pulling or gets distracted and disengages its attention, execute a 180-degree turn in the opposite direction, accompanied by a light tug on the leash. Continue to walk with purpose.

When the dog looks away, disengages, or tries to pull, TURN, TUG, and GO with purpose! Let this almost become a game.

> Be meaningful in your movements.

Surprise with Changes: The objective is to catch the dog off guard with sudden direction changes, providing a light, quick tug on the leash and turning in a new direction. This tug represents the applied "pressure" on the leash.

Pressure and Release: The tug and change in direction serve as the "pressure" points. Encourage the dog to respond by going with you, resulting in the "release" of pressure.

Ultimately, we want our dogs to respond to our leadership and become willing followers. They CHOOSE to walk with us.

Repeat the Drill: Continue the TURN, TUG, and GO sequence. Mastery is achieved when, despite the 6-foot leash, the dog instinctively moves with you without needing a tug. Incorporate this drill into your walks, employing it whenever the dog becomes distracted or attempts to pull—change directions, TURN, TUG, and GO.

This straightforward yet clear-cut drill teaches the dog a singular task: pay attention to the handler. If the dog diverts attention or disconnects, execute a surprising TURN, TUG, and GO. The once distracted and disconnected dog learns to keep an eye on you. Beyond working on the initial Point of Contact (POC) neck/leash pressure, the drill fosters an awareness of you as the Leader, someone of importance at the other end of the leash.

> Leaders need to be meaningful
> with their actions.

Once your dog seems to be dialed in and paying attention, this next drill can teach them to be even more hyper-aware of you and your personal space. Here's how it works:

Cut Through Drill

Turn Towards Them and Walk Through:

1. Position yourself to face the dog and walk directly through them, as if a line is drawn from you right through them.
2. Cut right into the space at their rib cage to drive them away.
3. Shuffle your feet with an attitude conveying, "Move out of my way!"

The objective is to encourage the dog to leave your personal space, gauging the necessary pressure. Use a calm, mildly invasive approach to drive the dog away, fostering the understanding that staying out of your space is desirable. This communication helps the dog maintain distance while moving with you during directional changes, setting the stage for advanced heeling drills.

We are teaching respect for our personal space. We are not trying to beat the dogs up or dominate them. Build the respect of YOUR personal space! Want to stop a dog from jumping on people? Teach them to respect human space. Step into them with assertive energy.

People who greet dogs with high energy encourage an invasion of their personal space. They are inviting the jump. Based on your actions, you have the dog you deserve. If you want to discourage jumping, be more thoughtful and purposeful when greeting a dog and demonstrate the boundaries by correcting the uninvited invasion of your personal space.

Combine with TURN, TUG, and GO Drill: Integrating these two drills systematically equips your dog to maintain focus, move with you, and respect your personal space. Use a fluid and confident motion with your TURN, TUG, and GO maneuvers. Begin with the entire 6-foot leash, gradually shortening the leash by making loops at the end to create a 5-foot and then a 4-foot leash. This progression will naturally position your dog at your side in a partnership, heeling position.

Combining TURN, TUG, and GO With the Cut Through Drill: Having mastered the Attention and Cut Through Drills independently, you now possess the tools to create a stress-free zone by your side—the ultimate partnership or 'heel' position. Focus on establishing this comfort or focus zone at your 3 o'clock or 9 o'clock (meaning on your right or left side). Change directions with TURN, TUG, and GO whenever the dog forges ahead. Gradually shorten the leash with one or two basketball-sized loops, increasing the dog's responsibility due to consequences when they pull against the leash.

> The objective is not to get your dog staring at you the whole time but to have a hyper-awareness of you. They are focused, thinking, and engaged and will be open to learning. Working dogs must be surveying their surroundings, but they can still pay attention to you.

Maintain a calm demeanor, responding promptly to the dog's actions. Encourage them to stay within the designated space on either side, "The Focus Zone," reinforcing the notion that the safest and most comfortable position is right by your side. The goal is to create a natural choice for the dog to be there without coercion.

It's crucial to keep hands light, yet your leash cues purposeful, rewarding the dog's efforts with a release of pressure. Repetition teaches the dog to pay attention to the handler and refrain from pulling on the leash. Over time, the dog learns to stay within a 6-foot radius, attentively following your movements and walking attentively at your side.

> It is not always about the pressure; it is often about backing off it.

Key Factors to Remember:

This training method utilizes the tug as an enforcer/ guide for cueing pressure and the release as a teaching moment. The handler guides the dog to seek comfort by responding to leash pressure, solidifying a strong connection, and being attentive. The dog voluntarily follows, understanding the consequence if they emotionally 'check out.' It becomes a mental game akin to "Simon Says," where they move in sync with your actions. Verbal language is minimized to maintain focus, with calm touches replacing excitable praise. This approach cultivates a calm, relaxed, and balanced demeanor, fostering leadership through mutual respect rather than stress, intimidation, or food bribery.

> They learn on the RELEASE!

Summary of Lease POC

In summary, the Leash POC is the cornerstone of a light-touch training system, teaching dogs to respond to meaningful pressure and cues applied to the leash. The ultimate objective is seamlessly transitioning this lightness to remote electronic collar cues for off-leash communication. While dogs quickly grasp the Point of

Contact (POC) concept, humans often struggle, applying excessive and ill-timed pressure.

Many handlers unknowingly bypass lightness, maintaining tight leashes akin to an aggressive hold rather than a polite, communicative greeting. This can lead to dogs wanting to escape or pull, as they never experience the reward of pressure release. Moreover, dogs are seldom taught to move away from pressure to release it, exacerbating the issue with harsher training devices.

> **Dogs move away from pressure. It is crucial to reward them with the release of pressure.**

Consistency is essential in dog training, emphasizing the importance of reinforcing the association between commands and desired actions. Rather than mindless repetition, a thoughtful approach involves teaching through cues and guidance, creating a language encompassing body language, leash cues, spoken words, and holistic communication. The goal is prompt responsiveness, especially when the dog's safety is paramount.

Next Steps To Create POC For Directional Cues

Creating a Point of Contact (POC) for directional cues involves building on the foundation of partnership established through the initial POC drills. The key is to keep your dog focused and engaged as their receptiveness to learning increases in such a state. The first stages of POC drills become a valuable tool for re-engaging your dog whenever they become disinterested or distracted.

Unbeknownst to you, the earlier drills, including TURN, TUG and GO, and the Cut Through Drill, have already laid the groundwork for essential commands such as "walk with me," "come to me," "be still," and "move away from me." When you stop, your dog learns to stop and observe you, anticipating a potential abrupt departure, reinforcing the concept of "be still." If they look or move away, there's a consequence. The TURN, TUG, and GO drill naturally instills the recall command as your dog approaches you in response. Stepping into your dog's space during the Cut Through Drill encourages them to move away, establishing the foundation for "move away from me" and the "join up" drill.

As a trainer who constantly seeks creative and enjoyable ways to enhance the training experience for both myself and my canine companions, I've developed a system that incorporates sending dogs to specific places. This method effectively refines and challenges the Point of Contact, adding a new dimension to the training process.

THE.QUIET.KUE™ CHALLENGE COURSE

The QK Challenge Course is an innovative approach to dog training that incorporates obstacles and training equipment into the leash and e-collar obedience program. This course was developed to add variety and challenges to the training routine, making it more engaging for both dogs and handlers. The obstacles also serve as a very easy-to-understand, straightforward, identifiable concept; you are either on or not on the obstacle. The goal is to use the leash POC to get the dog on, over, around, or through the obstacles.

> The Challenge Course is friendly to the people. When people see a task, they focus, and they calm down. The dogs then follow.

The QK Challenge Course provides dogs a structured environment with various obstacles and equipment, such as wobble boards, swinging bridges, truck beds, ladders, seesaws, balance beams, a rocking boat atop a truck tire, jumps, and more. These obstacles serve multiple purposes in the training program.

> The more challenges you can present,
> the better. The more challenges they learn
> to navigate, the more they understand.

Keep them and yourself fresh with new tasks and challenges.

Challenge and Variety: Basic leash training on flat ground can become monotonous for both dog and handler. Adding obstacles and challenges keeps training sessions exciting and mentally stimulating for both.

> The outcome of the obstacles:
> They learn that you are here to
> help them, NOT hurt them!

Building Confidence: Dogs are encouraged to navigate and interact with these obstacles, helping them build confidence in their physical abilities. This fact is particularly beneficial for dogs that may be timid or fearful. The obstacles present an exceedingly straightforward black-and-white challenge, and each dog must learn how to use their body and leg coordination to effectively navigate the course, all while being cued with the leash to encourage focus and willingness to try.

When Rick Smith first came to QK in 2015 and saw our challenge course, he was unconvinced. He thought it was just silly dog tricks. But then, Rick saw the magic happen. He noticed the PEOPLE gaining confidence and having a definitive task to tackle. He saw the PEOPLE become trainers. He witnessed the understanding, communication, and partnership being developed right before his eyes. Rick quickly became a fan!

Enhancing Leash Skills: The obstacles intensify leash resistance and unwillingness to follow light leash Point of Contact (POC) cues. Simple tasks such as stepping onto a platform when cued blow most dogs' minds! While these same dogs can easily scale countertops at home or jump on king-sized beds, they fall apart when you ask them to try these obstacles on our terms. This resistance can reveal a dog's threshold level and areas where they may need additional training to follow POC cues to go onto an obstacle.

Teaching Problem Solving: Dogs are challenged to think and problem-solve as they navigate obstacles. This mental engagement is an essential aspect of training. We use a task-oriented, systematic sequence to accomplish goals and navigate challenges. We also do dozens of valuable muscle and mind-building repetitions.

Building Trust and Partnership: Handlers guide dogs through the challenges using light yet directive POC cues. This technique builds trust and strengthens the partnership between the dog and the handler.

Promoting a "Try" Attitude: Instead of accepting a dog's resistance, the goal is to use light cues to create a "try" attitude. Correcting any attempts to resist or fight helps dogs make an effort and helps get rid of bailouts, meltdowns, and resistance behaviors. These often start with a refusal (freeze), a bolt (flight), then a bite on the leash (fight), jumping at the handler, and ultimately can present aggression when the dog cannot comprehend how to solve the problem. These reactions result from fear, lack of confidence, confusion, or an overindulged, coddled dog that never learned to face adversity because they were not required to complete simple tasks. The obstacles enable the handler to break down the reactions by setting clear boundaries. It is okay to fail, BUT you cannot flight, freeze, or fight.

> This is the stage where the people become the trainers. Determination and focus help people become more successful Leaders.

The Leader holding the leash will help you learn and succeed. Nearly every dog undergoing this process exhibits a beautiful, remarkable demeanor and body language change. A dog that learns to problem-solve, navigate even the most challenging obstacles, and succeed in portraying a fantastic posture of self-satisfaction acts like it just earned a blue ribbon. You can truly see and feel its glowing self-approval. It is happy, and it even prances!

Beautiful Behavioral Changes: Dogs' demeanor and body language often change significantly as they engage their brains and problem-solve. They become more confident, relaxed, and emotionally satisfied.

Yes, people will still be overwhelmed at times. These are simply wonderful opportunities to become better handlers. Sometimes, even if you are doing it wrong, you are still doing it right because you are doing SOMETHING. Be consistent, persistent, and patient, and success will follow.

Overcoming Reactivity: The QK Challenge Course has effectively reduced bite and bolt reactions in fearful dogs by helping them develop fundamental problem-solving skills. Sometimes, all that is needed is to simplify the challenge so that the dog is not so fearful. Build their confidence. But sometimes, it is best to attempt the most demanding challenges to face a dog that has learned to bite even when asked to face simple tasks.

While this often requires a skilled trainer, it has sometimes been an effective tool to address egregious, learned resistance tactics. Dogs' lashing-out reactivity must be corrected and redirected towards a try, not a fight or flight response.

Overly reactive dogs have yet to be asked to face challenges where they can seek success. Teach them the answer before you ask them the question. Don't try to fix the problem; the solution comes from your Foundation Training. Rather than correcting the wrong reaction, communicate the action that you want, for example, walk with me, come to me, be still, go, not NO!

Communication and Obedience: The obstacles are definitive objects to navigate, allowing for clear communication between the dog and the handler. The skills learned in the course can be applied to obedience training in various settings.

The challenging obstacles benefit ALL kinds of training, whether conformation, agility, fly ball, bird dogs, retrievers, herders, and especially pet companion dogs.

Proofing Obedience Cues: Handlers can use the obstacles to practice obedience cues, such as sending the dog to an obstacle, having them stay on the obstacle, or recalling them off it. This activity helps to teach and solidify the dog's response to verbal or hand signal commands.

Repetition and Muscle Memory: Dogs receive ample repetition and develop muscle memory in a structured and clear-cut manner through the course, making it easier to apply these skills in other situations.

In summary, The.Quiet.Kue™ Challenge Course is a valuable training tool that provides dogs with mental and physical challenges, builds confidence, strengthens the dog-handler partnership, and enhances obedience skills. Handlers can create their own course using readily available items to offer their dogs a stimulating and enriching training experience.

Looking around, our concrete and natural surroundings provide plenty of creative obstacles and challenges. From stone walls to park benches, tree stumps to slippery floors, and stairs to puddles, treat all these factors as your opportunity to challenge your leash POC and teach your dog to navigate these obstacles with the lightest of cues!

Let's Get Started with Sending to Obstacles

So, how can a simple elevated object help teach your dog better to understand the Point of Contact (POC) when lightly applied to its neck? Start with something definitive, like an elevated platform, box, or Kuranda-style bed.

The goal is to have a step or flat-topped, solid, and stable obstacle so your dog can easily step up and onto it. As you approach the obstacle with your dog on the

Wonderlead, apply persuasive, repetitive tugs on the leash towards it.

> Remember all the TURN, TUG, and GO ground drills we practiced to be still and walk with me? Well, you were setting the start of the Foundation to teach your dog to move away from the pressure or leash tugs. The obstacles further challenge and train a dog how to navigate the leash pressure by having a definitive TARGET to get on to.

In some cases, the dog may leap right up at the first attempt, and if this is the case, well done, but we need to find something more challenging. Follow this same process. For those dogs who put on the brakes, fight, freeze, or fly, here is your moment to teach!

Study the actions and feedback that your dog is giving you. Do they look away from the obstacle and pretend it is not even there? Do they freeze and not know what to do? Do they balk and try to get away? In these cases, use a cadence of light tugs towards the obstacle. Look for ANY effort of acknowledgment. This means dropping their head to look at it or sniff. A small step towards it. Even a slight lean towards it.

These are ALL tries, and if you pause to reward the try by simply stopping the cadence of leash tugs, this feedback rewards the dog for its try. The stopping of leash pressure is information that it made the right decision. It is essential to pause!

Remember to reward small successes!

While the goal is to get the dog onto the platform, the process involves a methodology of leash tugs to encourage the dog to follow the directional pressure toward the platform. They have four options:

1. Freeze and don't do anything
2. Flight and try to evade and get away
3. Fight by biting the leash or coming at you
4. Or lastly, they could try!

The first three actions are information that the dog does not understand that pressure is the enforcing, encouraging cue to follow. While I mostly rely on continuing with light leash tugs toward the obstacle, I will dig in harder for non-effort, especially for egregious actions such as bolting or fighting.

This response with my harder leash tug is information to make the WRONG action uncomfortable. With careful observation and timing, you can use assertive persistence to help cause a behavior change. If the change is positive and the dog gives a small try, the instant feedback is a reward for stopping the annoying tugs. If the reaction is egregious and they fight or bolt, then a quick, harder leash tug means, "Don't do that!" at which point I go back to my cadence of persuasive tugs.

Allow this process to play out because this is where you teach dogs to eliminate their fight, freeze, or flight resistance and instead give effort and try. Sometimes, the initial teaching takes the longest, and with each successive repeat of the drill applying light leash tugs toward the obstacle, the dog will learn how to follow the pressure and ultimately turn it off by moving with the leash guidance.

> Dogs begin to anticipate your ask and often offer the behavior before you even ask. This response shows that they understand your communication.

Once your dog succeeds with one obstacle, move on to a more challenging one. It may be small, less stable, or even scary. Use patience, persistence, and repetition as you did above each time. Encourage, reward small tries, and dig in a bit for egregious actions. These moments of resistance are your opportunities to teach. The release of pressure for the dog is the learning moment.

The reward is immediate once they are entirely on the obstacle, all four feet.

> Every dog will want to release themselves (pre-release), meaning they hop off before being cued off. This allowance puts the dog back in charge. Pay attention to the PRE-RELEASE!

If they leave the obstacle, repeat the process, ultimately envisioning that the obstacle is an 'island of comfort' and stepping off puts them in shark-infested waters. Help save them by teaching them to seek the island and stay there.

Staying on the obstacle becomes the Be Still action. This drill also works well sending your dog into their crate. Use the crate as a definitive island of safety and send them into it with light leash cues. One of my favorites is to use a 5-gallon bucket upside down and have them step onto the bucket with just light cues. Can you do this? If so, send us your QK Bucket Challenge photo, and we will post it on our social media pages.

As you continue to work on sending to obstacles, think about the underlying command you are trying to teach. Go away from me to a place to seek comfort.

Please realize that this is not normal for most of our dogs because they often have comfort by being clingy and at our sides as we pet them. They want to be near you, and now we are telling them to go.

Even for a dog that is a bolter (meaning it likes to run off), place training teaches it to go somewhere, and it indirectly helps to get rid of the flight response! The SEND teaches it to seek a destination and BE STILL.

Yes, it is part of the training process. So, be very aware that when you start to work obstacles, your goal is to use leash cues towards the obstacle and away from you. Can you stop before the obstacle and send them? If all your teachings have been walking your dog right to the obstacle, their learned muscle memory is more about heeling by your side and then getting on.

That differs from the goal; we want to send them, not walk them to it. What else can you do once they do it correctly? What drills or tasks can you come up with?

Try mastering the send from 4 feet, then 6 feet and 8 feet away. Face the obstacle, cue the leash towards and teach them to leave your side and go to the obstacle.

Now, find new obstacles and repeat this process to send and be still. Think:

Send away from you, stay there, and be still.

Dogs may need clarification on our next move. Will we walk, be still, or send them? They must pay attention, as our body language most often cues them even before the leash tug. They are learning to focus and problem-solve!

Next steps. Once they are on the obstacle and staying, what is the correct way to get them off and to make it another teaching moment? Here is where the recall, here or come command begins. Remember, we want to practice so many repetitions of sending them away that ultimately, the dog seeks the 'islands of pleasure' because they are safe spots. Staying on the islands feels good. Here is where many people teach that their movement is the sign to get off the island when we want to teach a leash CUE to get off the island. So it is essential to cue FIRST with the leash, and then you move to walk away; otherwise, your dog will release off of the obstacle on your movement rather than your leash cue.

How do you teach a dog to come? Teach them to go first! Every time your dog is safely on an island and learns that this spot is comfortable, it resists leaving the safe place. This response is part of the process; we are looking for this behavior. Why would they want to go into the 'shark-infested waters' if you are only going to send them back there anyway?

When I repeat the SENDING cues enough that dogs now show resistance to come off, I know that I have created a pattern in which they not only understand that a cue towards an obstacle means GO, but it also means chillax and BE STILL on that obstacle.

So, for my next task, I want to start to use decisive leash cues to guide and cue them to come to me. While you will experience initial confusion and resistance as they want to stay put, your persuasive tugs with well-timed releases for effort now begin to teach a new task: COME. You have already practiced this with your TURN, TUG, and GO drill; however, the goal is to work on communicating light leash tugs to cue the dog to leave the comfort and safety of the obstacle and come toward you.

Suppose you want to work on a recall from the obstacle that molds a come and a finished come to the heel position. This is a great time to teach with cues. Encourage them to come towards you as you back up and guide the dog's head inward towards you, their butt out as you draw them backward towards you; when their shoulder gets even with your knee, take a step forward, guiding them to your side so both of you are facing forward. This is effectively a backward J pattern if they are heeling on the left or a J if you guide them to the heel position by your side on the right.

The completed position is their shoulder by your knee and their front toes, even with your toes. Do this action; come to heel left and right with the J pattern.

By using a variety of obstacles to send, practice being still (staying on them), then recall off to heel by your side, you are creating dozens upon dozens of opportunities for leash cues and learning moments to SEND, BE STILL, COME, AND WALK WITH ME. You are practicing leash lightness to communicate The.Quiet.Kue™ system to teach your dog to follow a physical touch through your leash contact, verbal or even advanced-level nuanced non-verbal body language suggestions. At just the suggestive body language level, you are speaking on their terms through pack communication.

Watch your dogs communicate with each other. They do not speak! They use subtle cues and body positions in a comprehensive yet easy-to-observe language. When you pay attention, you can study the consistencies in their communication.

As you practice, you will start to notice patterns with your dog. An expected action is that they begin to seek the obstacles you have been practicing (even if just your crate that you have used repeatedly). We have nurtured and encouraged a lot of compulsion here. So you may find it challenging to even walk by that obstacle because the dog anticipates you are going to send him anyway, so he becomes an honor student and does the action EVEN BEFORE you ask him.

Wow, how clever and proactive of him! But this is also another wonderful teaching moment. Did you ask him to go, or did he go out of habit? As you refine your communication, look for these subtle moments where the dog was being proactive, anticipatory, and free-thinking, and they did the action before you cued. Use these moments not to correct or let them happen but instead as further moments to cue:

- Nope, stay by my side until I cue you to go.
- Or, Nope, I did not call you out of the crate even though I may have moved first.
- Wait for my physical cue to command you to come out.

These moments are learning opportunities, as habit and muscle memory can dictate much of your dog's actions and behaviors. Are they doing something because they 'always do' and that was their habit, or are they waiting for your cues to guide them?

The beauty of using various obstacles here is that not only does this present mental challenges where dogs need to partner with you and follow your guidance, but they also engage their brain to problem solve.

In addition, dogs' use of their core, hind ends, back muscles, and more to step onto, balance, and navigate sometimes unstable surfaces is an incredible physical workout, too!

As you master your leash POC, feel free to start adding a name to the actions. We like to use PLACE to send, HERE for the recall, HEEL for the walk with me, and either SIT/LIE DOWN or WHOA/STAY/WAIT for the be still. We do not use stay because if you ask a dog to SIT, that is the command. You should not have to repeat and nurture staying in SIT by repeating 'stay.' SIT means sit! So if they get up, command SIT again and reinforce with a leash cue.

The methodology for naming the actions can be done using your leash cue and naming the action as they are doing it. Be clear and say it once. Start to give the action a name. As the dog begins to hear this verbal command, think that the verbal is the lightest form of pressure you can provide.

The success behind the verbal commands lies in your ability to say the command once and then enforce the action with a leash cue. We do not want to start saying, HERE, HERE, HERE. Remember, with muscle memory and conditioning, they may decide that they only need to listen to your fourth HERE, and by then, they can already be in harm's way.

Since your command may be the lightest form of pressure, say it calmly. Let your tone be one of communication; never frustration, anger, or loudness while in this teaching and verbal conditioning mode.

We would much rather have the leash tug be the 'jerk' than you be a 'jerk' by yelling. You are to be the calm, composed LEADER!

Let's review. You have learned all about the Wonderlead as a training tool. You have learned valuable methods for correctly using the leash, and you have gone through a teaching process that makes it clear how to cue the dog to communicate. Nearly all of our leash work involves light cues to communicate a touch to guide a dog to complete an action. However, we have also integrated some harsher, well-timed leash tugs to correct some moments of egregious behavior.

Leash corrections may occur for jumping on you, bolting away or as part of the TURN, TUG, GO drill if you need to dig in a bit more to gain a dog's attention, etc. This 'in the moment' action using a leash tug correction is information that they are doing the wrong behavior. For the correction to be effective, it must change their behavior.

These corrections must be immediate and consistent whenever they try that unwanted behavior, clearly identify it, and be uncomfortable enough to deter it.

Regarding leash 'tug' corrections, the handler must be calm and assertive yet non-confrontational. You do not need to scare or intimidate. Let the LEASH be the JERK. Ill-timed or unclear corrections confuse and need to be clarified.

Inconsistent corrections for the same behavior are unfair and only reinforce the same bad behavior. Lastly, not digging in enough with a correction to stop the behavior may make a dog even more conditioned to endure the correction. As Rick Smith has taught me, "Sometimes you just need to go to a price they are unwilling to pay!"

TRANSITIONING TO OFF-LEASH TRAINING

Remote Training Collars

There is quite an array of remote electronic training collars out there. However, I am most familiar with and loyal to the once Tri-tronic collars, now owned by Garmin. I recommend the Sport Pro for family pets and the Pro 550 for larger dogs or field/sporting dogs. Garmin is synonymous with electronics, and the most critical factors in a remote e-collar are consistency, battery life, appropriate and variable stimulation levels, and integrity of the product to emit enough range at longer distances upwards of ½ mile. Just like our smartphones, you get what you pay for. The typical range for a quality e-collar is from $250 and up.

Anything less typically means you will not have the range or the power when needed. While these collars may ultimately save your dog's life, it is crucial to have them reliable!

"The e-collar doesn't teach. It cues them to do what they were already doing on leash." Rick Smith

While remote electronic training collars (e-collars) have faced much negativity and misinformation, they are invaluable tools when used correctly. Let's start by dispelling a common misconception: **these collars do not shock dogs.** Instead, they have two metal contact points that emit electronic pulses or continuous stimulation, ranging from extremely light to higher, uncomfortable levels. This stimulation is akin to a TENS transcutaneous electrical nerve stimulation unit, often used in human physical therapy, which generates a tingling sensation to reduce pain, relax muscles, and stimulate endorphin production.

It is widely employed in physical therapy, sports medicine, and for conditions such as arthritis. To clarify, electric shock is actually a sudden application of electric current that, when applied to the body with high strength and duration, can produce a convulsive response and potentially cause injury (Reilly, 1998). This is vastly different from the effects of an electronic training collar applied to the skin to contact superficial tissue (TENS). This stimulation will not burn the skin or cause electric shocks through the body.

For complete e-collar function, fit, and individual operation, please reference the instruction manual to use the brand and model you purchased. They are all slightly different, and you must use the correct contact point lengths with proper collar placement and fit.

In The.Quiet.Kue™ program, we introduce electronic collars after initial leash training. The foundation of POC (Point of Contact) cues, teaching dogs the four basic tasks of walking with us, staying still, going, and coming to us, typically takes several weeks of consistent work to ensure a solid understanding of these cues. Start to think about the methodology we have diligently been working on to teach and establish a point of contact.

We have carefully taught and conditioned our dogs to follow the lightest communicative cues with the leash. We have established a definitive POINT OF CONTACT that the dog can understand and follow. The hundreds upon hundreds of repetitive light leash cues now set the stage for the next level in lightness: cues with e-collar stimulation.

After the leash point of contact is completed, we introduce the electronic collar in conjunction with the leash. The aim is to use the collar's lightest possible setting, which produces a barely noticeable tingle sensation, serving as a gentle reminder when activated. This sensation might prompt a subtle response like a flicker of the ear, the dog glancing in the collar's direction, a momentary pause in panting, or even a blink of the eyes. The dogs are feeling *something*, and our goal is to communicate that the *something* is a new form of communication, soon to replace the leash touch and be your new form of off-leash cue communication.

The reaction is so faint that it is almost indiscernible. The success of your light leash communication has conditioned your dog to respond to lightness. The ultimate goal is to use extremely light pressure to communicate and elicit a response.

As you continue using The.Quiet.Kue™ of the leash, simultaneously incorporate the lightest possible electronic collar stimulation with a momentary **'nick'** of the electronic pulse. The dog's response is usually subtle, as the electronic collar merely offers a secondary cue to support your commands. This remote electronic collar conditioning process takes several weeks of consistent overlay, always in conjunction with the leash and dozens of daily repetitions.

> In reality, the amount of time it takes is the amount of time it takes. You are building upon a system from the Leash Point of Contact and teaching a new sensation in the form of an e-collar cue. The goal is to be thorough and consistent to truly build the Foundational language.

What is an e-collar 'nick' vs. 'continuous' stimulation? Many e-collars offer various options, from a rheostat dial to intensify the levels to a momentary or continuous button. With over 95% of our training, we want to use a 'nick' sensation as our touch point of contact. We use the continuous sparingly for higher levels as a meaningful correction to stop a behavior.

The leash guides movement and the electronic collar reinforces with the new 'nick' cue, teaching a new form of touch. With the four fundamental principles of walking with you, coming to you, staying still or stopping, and going to a designated place, you can perform numerous repetitions, particularly with obstacles, to integrate leash Quiet Kues with electronic collar nicks.

After consistently repeating leash POC cues and simultaneous electronic collar nicks, it's time to challenge your dog with situations that may tempt them to evade, escape, or give minimal effort where they do not seem genuinely engaged. These are moments where you can slightly increase the electronic collar intensity, promoting more significant commitment, focus, effort, compulsion, and determination to complete the task.

Increase at the moment as needed,
but ALWAYS return to the minimal,
lightest pressure your dog feels.

Once again, the leash guides while the electronic collar supports the cue. It simulates a 'leash tug' but with a different stimulus, motivating the dog to exert effort. The electronic collar stimulation ceases when the dog changes behavior to comply with your command or the leash guidance. The dog can halt the sensation of the electronic collar nicks by performing the requested command.

A simple concept: You make the proper behavior easy and the wrong behavior uncomfortable.

Here are some examples of when, how, and why to increase the electronic collar pressure:

Imagine you are walking your dog, and you halt to issue a cue with the leash and electronic collar. However, the dog sniffs the ground instead of complying and pulls or ignores your efforts.

As you cue and guide with the leash, you utilize a rhythmic sequence of electronic collar nicks (NICK pause one-one thousand NICK pause one-one thousand NICK). If, after 3 to 5 NICK electronic collar cues, the dog does not comply even with light guidance with the leash, you gradually and steadily increase the electronic collar intensity until the dog changes its behavior and follows the leash cue. Your leash cue guided the halt/stop by your side, and the e-collar pressure helped to support your leash cue.

Always remember you are in a position with the leash to guide the dog into action. By complying with the command, you reinforce and assist the dog in turning off the bothersome and mildly uncomfortable NICK pressure.

Be SLOW and RHYTHMIC. Nick, pause and wait for the response. Rewards efforts!

Remain very light with your leash cues! The leash guides the action; the e-collar stimulation is applied to direct them with a stronger cue.

The moment that they comply with your leash lightness, the e-collar cues cease.

This engagement of pressure is very similar to how we use cues with a horse. We often start first on the ground, teaching a horse to move away from pressure, but as we graduate to riding, it becomes another form of cuing. While in the saddle, you start with light seat (pushing your sit bone/butt) pressure on one side of your seat to move a horse sideways.

That is the lightest cue; next comes adding some leg pressure, next more leg with some touch of a heel or spur, and finally, if there is no attempt to move, you can engage a quick heel dig-in or spur (MOVE!).

This is a systematic sequence. The next time you ask, you again start with just your seat pressure and only escalate for a lack of try. You quit instantly when the horse gives you a try response. Interestingly, you cannot overpower a horse, but you can use cues to communicate and ask. When you identify and reward the little 'tries,' the animal learns to respond to the pressure with responsive effort.

Why not the same with dogs? We are stronger than our dogs, and we can force them to do a task; however, this means we are doing the work. The more we engage force in making them do something, the more they are no longer responsible for trying. Instead, they are being physically forced. Let's use more patience, teaching, and lighter cues of annoyance/mild discomfort, and when the dog chooses to find a solution and shows even a brief change in behavior, the pressure stops. The more animals understand how to turn the pressure off to discover the answer, the more they willingly comply, and we are not subduing them with force.

Tactics of a master trainer: Patience, persistence, repetition, teaching, reading the animal at the moment and responding, always willing to guide, encouraging, and being consistent. Set a standard and strive to uphold the basics and foundation as the building blocks of next-level training.

Precise timing is crucial to solidifying your dog's obedience and encouraging increased effort and focus. Reward any early efforts by ceasing the leash or electronic collar cue the moment they attempt. Conversely, communicate escape attempts with instant feedback, causing enough mild discomfort at the moment to change the behavior. Most dogs initially react to pressure with a flight, freeze, or fight response.

When they attempt these actions, promptly correct them with a leash jerk for trying to escape or evade, then resume guiding with the leash and cueing with the electronic collar. It's remarkable how swiftly a dog learns to cease evading and exert more effort to complete the task when it realizes their escape or fight response will be met with correction. For instance, if you ask a dog to climb into a new obstacle that may appear daunting, they might initially refuse by turning their head away, displaying escape denial.

Resistance becomes a habit. The bailout or "I can't" attitude becomes the default. When dogs learn to look away from an object, they express their unwillingness to try. They may be fearful, perplexed, or simply unwilling to attempt. While we recognize that it can be challenging or

frightening, not trying is not an option.
Training dogs to confront challenges
makes them significantly more confident,
courageous, and adept at problem-solving.

The 'Problem' is usually not the 'Problem.'
Instead, the lack of foundational
skills provides the answers about
what to do right (heel, be still, go, or
come) rather than trying to correct
the reactive or wrong behavior.

Dogs are intelligent creatures who must learn to confront adversity and solve problems, not evade them. The
act of escaping or bailing out can easily be nurtured to
the point where a dog cannot climb stairs, enter a car,
walk on shiny floors, step onto a vet's table, and so forth.
They are denied the opportunity to learn. Instead, they
are coddled and enabled to the extent that they become
insecure, fearful, and incapable of success. I consider this
dog 'dumbed down' by his humans because they lack the
essential problem-solving skills to navigate life.

These same dogs are often fearful, obstinate, unstable, or aggressive. They have been denied the opportunity to reach their full potential and a higher quality of

life. Frequently, I hear owners saying the dog won't listen, has anxiety, or cannot be trained.

In reality, this dog never had the opportunity to truly learn.

When you promptly respond with a leash correction when a dog opts for the escape, making their action uncomfortable, it is astonishing how often they will attempt the task you requested. The simple rule here is to make the wrong response complex or challenging and the right choice easy.

Dogs are brilliant at picking up on non-verbal cues, and it's often the most effective way to communicate with them. It's like developing a silent dance between you and your pup. The leash becomes a subtle guide, your body language a nuanced conversation.

I was recently handed a wild eight-month-old Brittany pup, where the owner said she is crazy, hyper, and doesn't listen. Sure enough, she rushed her 35-pound frame at me, pulling him all of the way on a 20-foot-long cotton leash. She was to be my next field dog project. I promptly stepped into her and at her as she rudely tried to take me out and jump. I then calmly took over the leash. When she then attempted to bolt away (I guess that I was not a fun victim!), I gave her a tug back towards me. My energy commanded calm confidence, and my attitude portrayed assertive Leadership. I had her leash, and I was in control. I swiftly made her bolt reactions uncomfortable with a leash tug and release, yet I assertively stepped into her if she came within a hula hoop of my space. In about 30 seconds of me making her wrong actions difficult and her right ones easy (when she stopped, I stopped and stood still), she immediately chose to lie down and politely wait while her owner told me all her bad habits and problems. She and I both intently listened to the list of her issues. She never moved. She then happily trotted off to my truck with me, happy to have a Leader at the other end of her leash!

Quietly teaching through actions and cues makes the training more intuitive for the dog and encourages the trainer to be more observant and responsive. It's a two-way street of understanding.

Navigating a dog's reactions and responding appropriately is a skill that aligns seamlessly with effective training. Once this foundational communication is established, the logical progression is to assign a name to the command. It's akin to adding words to a language they already comprehend.

Through consistent repetition, your dog develops muscle memory and conditioned responses to essential commands: go, stop, come, and with me. As you introduce verbal cues, your dog can exert effort in compliance.

CANINE COMMUNICATION

Your body language IS a form of communication. How does your dog understand what the e-collar cues mean without verbal cues? This is a widespread question. When reviewing all of the steps you took to achieve leash cues, your body language also tells a story. For instance, if you were facing an obstacle, your focus and energy would cue the dog to address the object. Your step toward the obstacle would also be a cue. Being silent helps to encourage you to use your body to cue—you just were not realizing it! If you moved away, your energy said, 'Come with me.' If you stopped, your energy said, 'Be still.' Remember, dogs are masters of reading body language. They pick up on your physical cues even before the verbal ones. So, think of using your body to communicate.

> The handler must focus. This, in turn, focuses the dog.

Imagine that you have an inner force to push and send them away, a soft, welcoming force to draw them into you, an energetic and join-up force to have them walk with you, and a calm force to nurture the stop. This is ultimately your Quiet Communication that supports the physical touch. If you apply a leash or e-collar cue, your dog has had enough previous situational repetition of GO, COME WITH, STOP, OR COME TO ME through the use of obstacles.

If your dog doesn't respond to verbal commands, initiate e-collar nicks in a rhythmic sequence until effort is observed. Increase intensity if necessary. If compliance remains elusive, guide with the leash. Yet, discern whether your dog is genuinely confused, stuck, or obstinate—reading your dog is an essential skill developed through training, coaching, and diligence.

A common problem with voice commands is that people's actual body language often overrides the verbal, while the body language frequently instructs the opposite. Stepping into or at a dog drives them away, yet how many people bend slightly at the waist (which is threatening) with aggravated energy and step towards their dog to command them to come? Would YOU want to go to that energy? Additionally, each person uses a different tone, voice inflection, and cadence when they speak. So if I spend thousands of repetitions teaching YOUR dog MY verbal cues, that becomes their muscle memory. It is challenging to have you repeat the verbal language that I created. Therefore The.Quiet.Kue™ is a system that teaches with touch through a leash or e-collar as the language. The owner can then name the actions whatever they want, in whatever language they like, by transitioning their unique language in association with The.Quiet.Kue™ system.

Always prioritize helping your dog, but if you sense distraction or obstinance to a specific command, systematically escalate the e-collar cues to a level they find uncomfortable. This makes ignoring leash guidance less appealing. Ensure the right action is easy and comfortable, while the wrong one is associated with mild discomfort. The ultimate aim is to transition smoothly to using only the lightest communication, which can include body language, hand signals, voice commands, or physical touch at points of contact.

Command with your verbal (sit). What is the response? Remember, the dog needs to hear, process, and react. No further pressure is required if he sits; perhaps a gentle, rewarding touch. If there is no effort, initiate e-collar nicks alongside gentle leash guidance, gradually increasing the e-collar intensity until your dog shifts behavior and aligns with the leash guidance. Consistency and repetition will, as always, lead to your dog responding to verbal cues, requiring occasional e-collar reminders to enforce or intensify compliance. Prioritize noticeable effort over speed in your training approach.

Always look for appropriate effort for each dog. Effort is a try! It may be slow, but they need to hear, think, process, and then act upon your questions.

In this phase, remember that your dog needs time to process and act upon your verbal commands. Approach the training slowly, patiently, and calmly, speaking clearly and authoritatively. Keep your voice softer than the pressure from the leash or e-collar, letting the tools be the 'jerks'—leash jerks or e-collar nicks. You are the composed leader utilizing tools to teach, guide, and correct.

Ultimately, your verbal command is the lightest form of communication, but the e-collar and leash are also alternative forms of communication. The DIFFERENCE is that you can intensify the physical pressure with a leash or e-collar point of contact. We want to refrain from intensifying our verbal commands! If your dog does not respond to your initial verbal command, systematically go through the next phase with leash guidance lightly along with e-collar nicks as your light cue.

Anytime that you incessantly repeat verbal commands, you are conditioning your dog that it is ok to ignore the first commands. Think about how they MUST respond to your emergency HERE command if they are running out towards the road. Condition them in this training phase so that when they do not react to your verbal cues, they receive a leash and e-collar stimulus as a reinforcing consequence.

Don't overthink it! The leash guides the actions, and the e-collar helps to cue. They work in conjunction and support each other. We ultimately want dogs to listen to the verbal, the leash, and the e-collar. So, all three are forms of communication. They are your three tools. The leash and e-collar touch are simply forms of physical communication.

As you progress, you'll find that, with a well-established foundation using quiet cues and leash guidance, the verbal command alone prompts action. This is the moment—you've transitioned from leash cues to e-collar cues. In the next phase, consider using a lightweight, long line for backup or practicing off-leash commands in a controlled environment.

If your dog fails to comply, even with e-collar cues, default to helping them. Use two or three increasing e-collar nicks, maintain the sequence, and guide with the leash to ensure success. The entire process, leash Point of Contact (POC) to e-collar POC to off-leash transition, will take the time it takes based on your commitment to consistent lessons, repetitions, proofing, and practice. We want to teach a new language and test and prove it in various environments, situations, and distractions. There is no need to put a time frame on it and rush. The more you teach and practice, the better you and your dog will form a new level of communication and partnership.

Many people make the prevalent mistake of stopping use of the e-collar. For some reason, they see this as a negative and only use it if necessary. I'm afraid that's not right because the e-collar is a language that must be practiced. Can you quietly cue and communicate non-verbally with your dog just with the e-collar? Continued practice and proofing are crucial. Proofing involves introducing higher distractions, such as other dogs or people. In such situations, be prepared to increase leash or e-collar pressure to regain focus.

> Always return to the lightest
> physical cue your dog can feel.

Proofing also exposes dogs to potential escape routes, such as bolting back home or towards distractions that momentarily captivate them more than their desire to comply. This phase is a normal part of training, as dogs sometimes reach their limits or succumb to high distractions. These moments are valuable learning opportunities—address the escape attempt and reinforce completion of the command.

> Train for those wrecks! We WELCOME those opportunities for even better training. While some instances may feel like you are setting your dog up for failure, they are also opportunities to help dogs grasp that higher pressure levels should create more significant effort and compulsion. COME HERE NOW! If a dog resorts to fight, freeze, or flight under intensified e-collar or leash pressure, it indicates a lack of understanding in turning off the pressure. Their resistance could stem from fear, confusion, obstinance,

> or dominance. Regardless, the training
> goal is to navigate this resistance toward
> a state of compliance, communication,
> and partnership with your dog.

In reflecting upon people's challenges of being so married to being vocal and needing verbal communication, I think about the many clinics where I asked participants with intermediate to advanced dogs to switch dogs with another handler. Suddenly, those who may have had a beautiful harmony and verbal language with their dog needed to really focus, go back to the basics and become trainers again. People had to try different ways to help the dogs understand them, and most often, they fell right back to the leash cues to build the communication because the dog did not understand their unique verbal sounds or even odd body language. There also was a shift in the handler's demeanor because the dogs needed guidance, and the handlers needed to focus, slow things down, and read the dog they had at the moment.

ELIMINATING TRASH BREAKING BEHAVIORS

The e-collar is a correction tool in specific situations, particularly in what is commonly known as "Trash Breaking." While 95% of our communication through the e-collar involves subtle cues for guidance, there are critical moments where a higher level is warranted to deter a dog from potentially dangerous actions.

Trash breaking, although an abrupt correction, is not aimed at causing lasting pain but rather making a significant impression. The e-collar's impact, even at its highest setting, is minor compared to the potential dangers averted—such as ingesting harmful substances or chasing into traffic.

APPROACHES TO TRASH BREAKING

Setting Off-Limits Boundaries:
For behaviors like counter surfing, establish an 'off-limits' boundary **WITHOUT** your presence.

- Place high-value food at the counter's edge, observing from a hidden vantage point.
- Without verbal correction, let the dog approach. When the dog intends to jump (nose up sniffing, get ready!). Let them make a definitive move—to

jump, then apply a high-level continuous e-collar correction for 2 seconds.

To catch them in the moment, let them commit to the crime. Then correct!

- Though scary, surprising, and uncomfortable, this method imparts an immediate and decisive consequence, deterring the dog from the action.
- While it might be challenging to watch, this setup is a proactive measure to safeguard your dog's life from potential hazards on counters, such as medications and packaged food.

This method is versatile and can be applied to behaviors like carrying rocks, eating feces, accessing the litter box, raiding the garbage, or jumping onto windows.

The ultimate goal of this approach is to discourage the dog from engaging in these actions, prioritizing their safety and well-being. They also learn that they need to hold accountability and responsibility to stay away from these dangers even in your absence.

Trash Breaking Method Two:
Marking the behavior **WITHIN** your presence:

The second approach to trash breaking involves marking the behavior before issuing a correction. This valuable training method employs a cue (verbal or e-collar tone) to signal a warning before the corrective action. This method informs the dog that their current action is unacceptable, and consequences will follow, and they MUST follow! Example: Dealing with a chronic poop eater.

- Identifiable Marker: In the moment of the action, use a consistent and authoritative marker. For instance, say "LEAVE IT" with emphasis.
- Immediate Correction: Immediately following the verbal marker, issue an appropriate correction during the training phase. The goal is to empower the command "LEAVE IT" with a tangible consequence.
- This command extends beyond curbing undesirable behaviors like eating feces—it becomes a powerful tool applicable to various situations, from interacting with human guests to avoiding places they shouldn't explore (e.g., litter box, coffee table with food).

Building Power:
Providing an appropriate correction after issuing the command strengthens its impact. The ultimate aim is for the dog to associate "LEAVE IT" with the anticipation of correction, even when you can't physically correct them.

The Invisible Fence System Comparison

This marking concept bears a resemblance to invisible fence systems. During the training phase, the boundary is marked with flags. Dogs are brought close to the boundary, and a correction follows a collar warning tone if they persist. During this training phase, the dogs are on a leash, and when they approach the flags and hear the tone, they are purposely pulled into the invisible fence and receive quite a high level of correction.

At this moment, the fence boundary trainer will pull the dog back inside the boundary so that they learn how to turn the pressure off and stay safe and contained. This process is repeated along several boundary areas to teach the dog first with a visual flag and then with the warning tone; then, they must feel the pain when they venture into the fence. Fences are set to a higher level to inflict pain because the consequence must be a strong deterrent from high-value distractions such as running squirrels, other dogs, or anything that may highly entice them to chase.

Feeling the discomfort of the boundary teaches them to avoid it, seeking comfort by stepping back into the safe yard area. This is corrective training and while the intensity level is high, nothing can compare to the impact of being hit by a car because the dog did not respect the fence boundary.

Dogs not systematically taught this training might challenge the fence or fail to understand the boundaries, leading to avoidance or fear of the yard. Proper training ensures they know and respect the boundaries and freely enjoy the safe space within.

Trash Breaking Across Behaviors: A Moment of Impact

Whether it's trash, digging, barking, or chasing a deer, there are moments when a swift and impactful correction is necessary. However, long, continuous, surprising, and uncomfortable corrections can trigger a flight response. Typically, if YOU are using the e-collar with emotions of anger or frustration, you have failed. For example, when calling a dog to come, escalating immediately to a high e-collar level might cause them to bolt. Instead, start with light e-collar nicks, gradually increasing until compliance is achieved, always reverting to the lightest level afterward, which is the verbal recall command.

One crucial note: never employ a high-level e-collar correction in cases of aggression toward humans or other dogs. High arousal states can intensify with such corrections, and they are not suitable for surprising corrections near people, potentially leading to reactive behavior.

Remember, the e-collar can successfully be used to halt actions—whether it's an "Ouch," a pause, or a complete stop—it is unsuitable for aggressive situations, especially when a dog is highly agitated or aroused (red zone).

The E-Collar as a Valuable Training Tool

When used in harmony with a leash program, e-collars provide off-leash communication that enhances a dog's quality of life. The freedom to run, play, and explore off-leash becomes a safer joy when coupled with the assurance and ability to enforce recalls, and maintain control in potentially dangerous situations.

Best Practices:

Methodical Use: During the training phase, consistently use e-collars with a leash program.

Continuous Wear: During the conditioning phase, keep the collar on throughout the day. Avoid only putting it on for training sessions or reactive behavior.

Avoiding Collar-Wise Behavior: Regular use prevents dogs from associating the collar only with training sessions or being used to correct rather than low-level communicative cues, ensuring they listen consistently. Refrain from displaying the remote with a threatening attitude (it is not a TV remote control, so don't pick the remote up and point it at the dog like it has magic laser beams coming out of it! Be nonchalant). The BEST way to teach a dog to be collar-wise is to not have the collar on when you need it, so you put it on after the dog's infractions and try to correct or repeat it. This teaches the dog to listen only when the collar is on. Do NOT make this mistake!

Despite this coaching, I still cannot believe how many clients tell me, "All I have to do is pick up the remote and point it at them, and they listen." Or "Funny, he only listens with his e-collar on" (OK, then be more consistent and keep the e-collar on during his waking hours and off at night). Or, "He acts pouty when I put the collar on; he hates that collar."

These comments clearly show that the owner is NOT using the collar properly, consistently, or as light cues. The dog will forget the language if you stop practicing light cue communication.

Building Respect: The goal is for the dog to respect you and your commands, viewing the collar as a safety measure akin to a seat belt or insurance policy.

Post-Training Use: Even after completing the training phase, continue using the collar for several months to ensure consistent response to verbal cues. Periodically practice e-collar cueing language to reinforce their application and even challenge at times for greater compulsion.

High-Distraction Situations: The collar remains a valuable enforcement tool in high-distraction settings or situations demanding immediate recall (public parks, near roads).

Please think of the e-collar as a tool that, when used thoughtfully, fosters a deeper bond and understanding between you and your canine companion, providing a safety net for their well-being and freedom.

Will I always need an e-collar? Most likely not; however, why not view it as an insurance policy any time your dog is off-leash? There are so many potential dangers out there, and the e-collar gives you immediate communication and control, which could save your dog's life.

CONCLUSION

The.Quiet.Kue™ represents the culmination of three decades of training. This journey has been shaped and inspired by the wisdom of my mentors and coaches and the invaluable lessons taught by countless dogs. Many of these incredible dogs have reaped the benefits of my commitment to helping them.

In contrast, others have patiently witnessed my learning curve, which involved making mistakes, evolving, and refining my toolbox of techniques. Each dog is unique, and I deeply cherish the hands-on experience I've gained while building my Quinebaug Kennels business. I've had the privilege of training hundreds of remarkable animals throughout my career.

I profoundly appreciate and respect all animal training methods that employ systematic, fair, and humane approaches to educate animals, enabling them to live harmoniously and happily within our human world. The success stories that result from these methods are genuinely heartwarming. The.Quiet.Kue™ methods have consistently demonstrated their effectiveness, proving to be a valuable training tool for dogs with diverse backgrounds and needs, whether they've suffered from neglect or abuse, exhibited aggression or instability, or been cherished family companions or high-level competitive sporting dogs.

I take great pride in sharing these methods with fellow dog professionals, offering precise guidance for targeted problem-solving. Moreover, I've simplified these techniques to make them accessible and practical for novice dog owners and even young children. In simple terms, The.Quiet.Kue™ system works. I eagerly anticipate hearing about your success stories. I am truly honored to have shared ideas and training methods that enhance your communication, leadership, and relationship with your dog.

Trained Dogs Live Better Lives

ABOUT THE AUTHOR

Jennifer Broome is a distinguished figure in the realm of dog training, renowned for her expertise in sporting dog training and obedience. With a lifelong passion for dogs and the outdoors, Jennifer founded Quinebaug Kennels in 2001, leveraging her wealth of experience and dedication to providing top-notch training, boarding, grooming services, breeding, and canine wellness services. Her journey began with humble beginnings in dog walking and pet sitting, gradually evolving into a full-time career centered on nurturing well-trained canine companions.

Jennifer's extensive background includes a degree in Wildlife Biology and Management from the University of Rhode Island, complemented by hands-on experience in breeding and training Labrador Retrievers and German Shorthaired Pointers. Her commitment to excellence led her to transition to full-time dog training and boarding services, where she has excelled as a talented trainer and kennel owner.

Jennifer's prowess extends beyond traditional obedience training, as evidenced by her remarkable achievements in sporting dog competitions such as AKC retriever hunt tests, field trials, and conformation shows, as well as the NAVHDA testing system. She was also a pro-staff trainer for Cabela's for 10 years, traveling the country to teach and do demonstrations with her dogs.

With a keen focus on honing the skills of hunting dogs, she has earned a stellar reputation as a sought-after authority in the field. Committed to continuous learning and improvement, Jennifer actively collaborates with renowned figures in retriever, spaniel, and pointing dog training, as well as sporting dog wellness, fitness, and nutrition. She remains dedicated to sharing her expertise with fellow trainers and clients.

RESOURCES

Quinebaug Kennels (QK)

The world-class epicenter of canine care and wellness.

Based in beautiful Northeast Connecticut, QK's ongoing vision has been responsible for its prestigious reputation. This reputation was earned through its steadfast dedication to a quintessential, proprietary philosophy known as The.Quiet.Kue™.

With 50 acres hosting what they do and used to show the world how they do it, they focus daily on one simple, collective goal: the all-encompassing, long-lasting well-being of their guests.

Few are the places that strive to deliver thoughtful & responsible dog care and training in a manner that considers the continuing wellness of visiting dogs. From enacting a set of beliefs where soft touches and observations achieve a higher, unparalleled level of successful communication, to create the most peaceful of partnerships.

From complete sporting and companion training events and seminars to short- and long-term responsible boarding, proper care-centric grooming, and an array of complete rehabilitation services. From their prized (and highly-demanded) opportunity known as Vita Plena to their ability to care for senior dogs using nearly 30 years of experience in appropriate elderly dog care.

Today, many believe QK is one the few places left where they ensure a dog will genuinely live their life to the fullest…either while visiting or once they've arrived back home. https://www.qkdogs.com/

Artistry Afield

A sporting and conservation opportunity enhancing everyone's storybook life afield.

Founded by Jennifer Broome, a lifelong sportswoman, Artistry Afield encourages passionate, like-minded sporting enthusiasts to reach further and engage in sporting moments and opportunities afield unlike any other. As Jennifer puts it so well, "I wanted to offer our clients something uncommon and unique while also offering them the opportunity to learn something new that would move their passions forward."

Today, Artistry Afield is offering a line of self-designed field gear and accouterments, exclusive sporting global travel destinations, and world-renowned, foundational puppy training, enabling sportsmen and sportswomen to ensure the best life afield next to their four-legged friend.

When it comes to their private product line, their teams' vast experience sourcing the finest raw materials and envisioning invaluable features in products uncommon in today's markets is just one reason why Artistry Afield is augmenting the finest moments lived outdoors. https://www.artistryafield.com/

DEVOTION SUPPLEMENTS

QK's All Natural and Proprietary Supplement Line Enabling Your Dogs Best Health & Well-Being

Envisioned and created at QK, the state-of-the-art epicenter of canine care and wellness in Northeast Connecticut, DEVOTION is a proprietary line of all-natural supplements designed to maximize dogs' overall nutrition.

As one may agree, a dog is what they eat, and it is clear those who show dull coats, weakened immune systems, allergies, or lick and eat dirt, rocks, or poop are not getting adequate nutrition. Being a proprietary line of fresh, quality-forward ingredients, each bag is made to order, enabling peace of mind to all those DEVOTED to their dogs.

Daily Support +: Daily Support + supports your dog's skin, coat, digestive system, and more with a daily vitamin/mineral boost and a healthy dose of natural Omega-3. It also contains custom-blend Probiotics and Probiotics providing comprehensive joint support for active, working dogs, and older dogs with joint support needs.

Norwegian Dried Kelp: This underwater seaweed contains at least 25 vitamins, including vitamins A, B12, and folic acid, and aids in maintaining a shiny coat and healthy skin. Rich in vitamin D, calcium, iron, iodine, potassium, sulfur, and magnesium, kelp also contains sodium alginate, which is said to rid the body of heavy metals and radioactive elements.

Digestive Wellness: A unique blend of Prebiotics, Probiotics, and digestive Enzymes, it optimizes the absorption of nutritional supplements for overall improved health and well-being. It also stimulates and feeds beneficial intestinal bacteria.

The Delmar Smith Wonderlead: "You'll Wonder How You Lived Without It!"

The Quiet.Kue™ book is a comprehensive explanation of Wonderlead's history, background, and operation. It is the most effective training tool for creating a Point

Of Contact to achieve lightness with the leash and provides the best Foundational Training for later e-collar conditioning. This special lariat-style tool is often imitated but never duplicated! Purchase online from our QK Store. https://www.qkdogs.com/shop

www.akc.org
Whether you're a breeder or a new dog owner, AKC is the trusted expert for all things dog. Learn about the breeds, dog sports and events, find breeders, and learn about the most up to date health and wellness for dogs.

www.akcchf.org
Canine Health Information Center, also known as CHIC, is a centralized canine health database jointly sponsored by the AKC Canine Health Foundation (CHF) and the Orthopedic Foundation for Animals (OFA). CHIC, working with participating parent club, provides a resource for breeders and owners of purebred dogs to research and maintain information on the health issues prevalent in specific breeds. Browse this site to see if the dog breed and breeder that you are interested in is currently enrolled in the CHIC program and what tests are required to obtain a CHIC number.

www.catooutdoors.com
Dog training platforms made in the United States. Safe, elevated, sturdy, portable and stackable. Once your dog understands "Place" on the Cato Platforms, you have a

new gateway to good things! The Cato Platform can be used for almost any scenario – visitors at the door, control when being let in or out, feeding time, remote sits, recall, steadiness training, handling drills and upland field drills. With a little patience and creativity, the Cato Platforms will change the way you interact with your dog!

www.garmin.com
The leader in the industry for remote electronic collars for family pets and sporting dogs. From training and bark-reducing collars to GPS tracking systems, their comprehensive line of collars encompasses a vast array of sizes, styles and options.

www.healthypawspetinsurance.com
Top rated pet insurance. Available in all 50 states, Healthy Paws Pet Insurance has been rated #1 based on customer reviews for over 7 years in a row. Covering accidents, illnesses, cancer, emergency care, genetic and hereditary conditions, breed-specific conditions and alternative care.

www.huntsmith.com
Celebrating over 50 years of helping people train their field and bird dogs.

www.kuranda.com
Dog beds that are orthopedic, chew proof and easy to clean. Kuranda's elevated dog beds provide a great relief

for dogs' joints. The cot style design evenly distributes their weight so there are no pressure point like they would have on the ground. Kuranda's patented design secures the fabric side the frame making it totally inaccessible to dogs that chew. Guaranteed for 1 full year. Unlike pillow style beds that hold odor and hair, these beds can be hosed or wiped to clean. Accessory pads are machine washable. At Quinebaug Kennels, Kuranda Beds are our #1 choice for our kennel bedding AND they are a staple for our training programs providing an elevated, distinctive, identifiable platform to "Go Lie Down". Additionally, the bed is serves as a destination for "PLACE" whether you use the bed indoors or outside on the patio to provide a definitive platform to stay on.

www.ofa.org
Orthopedic Foundation for Animals mission is to promote the health and welfare of companion animals through a reduction in the incidence of genetic diseases.

www.purina.com
Nestlé Purina PetCare creates richer lives for pets and the people who love them. Founded in 1894, Purina has helped dogs and cats live longer, healthier lives by offering scientifically based nutritional innovations. Purina manufactures some of the world's most trusted and popular pet care products, including Purina ONE, Pro Plan, Fancy Feast and Tidy Cats. Our more than 10,000 U.S.

associates take pride in our trusted pet food, treat and litter brands that feed 46 million dogs and 68 million cats every year. More than 500 Purina scientists, veterinarians, and pet care experts ensure our commitment to unsurpassed quality and nutrition.

Purina promotes responsible pet care through our scientific research, our products, and our support for pet-related organizations. Over the past five years, Purina has contributed more than $150 million towards organizations that bring, and keep, people and pets together, as well as those that help our communities and environment thrive.

REFERENCES

Battaglia, C. L. (n.d.). *Building Better Breeders*. Early Neurological Stimulation | Breeding Better Dogs. https://breedingbetterdogs. com/article/early-neurological-stimulation

Kerns, N. (2021, March 30). *The no-pull harness debate*. Whole Dog Journal. https://www.whole-dog-journal.com/care/collars-harnesses-leashes-muzzles/the-no-pull-harness-debate/

Reilly, J. P., & Reilly, J. P. (1998). *Applied Bioelectricity: From electrical stimulation to electropathology*. Springer.

www.ingramcontent.com/pod-product-compliance
Lightning Source LLC
LaVergne TN
LVHW051251080426
835513LV00016B/1852